Know Your Country

Know Your Country

Kerri Shying

PUNCHER & WATTMANN

First published in 2021
Published by Puncher and Wattmann
PO Box 279
Waratah NSW 2298

http://www.puncherandwattmann.com
puncherandwattmann@bigpond.com

NATIONAL
LIBRARY
OF AUSTRALIA

A catalogue entry for this book is available from the National Library of Australia.

ISBN   9781925780765

Cover design by Miranda Douglas
Typesetting by Morgan Arnett
Printed by Lightning Source International

Contents

for Cosmo Chambers and Tegan Rowney,
my whole heart and best supporters

talented regardless

can you just exist   to exist   or am I just thinking now of
organizations for the poor   I get confused when I drift through

the reasons to speak at all   on the one hand   people laugh and
clap their hands on the other   the sound   of burrs being taken

off of knives   and the thump of hessian onto truck beds   reminds
me nothing   lasts forever I speak   before   the bliss that hangs

a half-drunk halo   about the head of admiration hardens into
incapacity   then clatters   shatters splays a trail   behind me

running   .

can I be the me in me   or am I made of what has come before
who that made me   how they say me am I that or is there more

heirlooms

once upon a time

there were three suns
blazing in the one sky

each one arguing
over what

shade of blue might
suit them best

it was the gambling
autocrat   who thought to cage them

up

online the clickbait the
stuck-together friends

shared and tagged
a'bicker in corral

in my day they roamed
among the generations free

stomped us into families
hunting fighting gathering

not now

autocracy

hate the people   make up   part of me   I hate
the people   make up   things   I left behind   might

have been a part of all the   ladder-climbing
rock-wall grabbing   panoply of myth   class fighter

here in this now space   in this   not virtual real
reality   I can say it was the day   they   shot a monkey into space

left us suckers   here behind   to race   obliterate
me   cringing   fingernails on blackboard   odd

walk beside it   and you die
remember that   fifth grade

year all the girls avoided

you and your Italian face my
problem the same colour hair

as the one they called the breed
I hate the part of this   I see

in me

in my skin

it's a Dulux colour chart of skins
my kin
I love

from merging with the bookcase
to flaming out the light meter

all the one mob here
oh   how colossal
the right
that courses through the veins   of every total prick
that questions who we are

assimilation
is the kind of turd who smacks you in the mouth
then says
get up   you're bleeding on the carpet

mate
as if
as if   but
rebuttal
puzzle pieces   whittled by a thumbless monkey

always there
and giving pause
that calloused grudge of less proud skins
takes long glance up   and hard glance down
and speaks   the iteration of all fear
my fault   my loss   a million cracks that lead to country towns
and saloon bars

shame recast to pride offends

generations of debate

I am left here
in one sock   coated with the dust   picking up the chip packets
rounded on with a pointed finger

well you started it

just can't get her act together

go ask the lantana   why
her flowers come in varied hues

bar her   if you want to
keep an eye out for those bees

they hang around

don't
spread your toast with honey
either

that mouth best be open mate
to breathe

galmalngidyalu nhal gaghaanggilinya

(the song delights me)

gunya is my first word   hear cunjevoi
pak ah pu   the gidgiman
   words are lands and faces   special
tucked inside

my nanna   when we travelled
would say   who are your people
on the day train   down to Melbourne
we would ask the ones around us
where's your country   who's your people
i expect you know the rest

the crossing is the telling   and the moving
is the seeing   the sore bums and the cold pies
of the strangers on the rail

a million tonnes of ballast sang out a song beneath me
a million tonne extracted from the soil of everywhere

it called to us in rocking throat
the state the state the state

see   all one field of grey
she says   look closer   there
where brown   abuts the
tan and touches black us resting on steel
blue

the Perway is one item made of all our knowing

each vibration strums   the covalent
in its fellow   hear it announcing

its rapacity   speaking out
the capacity   the waves
and troughs   a whisper   revelation
signals
stone to stone

rocking lulling damping
our whereabouts each moment
beneath the sleepers telling
what belongs to where

I hold tight to all her stories given
to me moving mouth to
ear   mouth to ear mouth
to ear

yama-ndhu gulbarra?
do you understand?

remind me

what did you look like
when you were young did you have

black hair red hair were you blonde
was that tip-tilted chin a match with

balled rose cheeks   now grey snails
crawl across our heads steal the

views   munch it up   this
old paper   leave the string

shanghaied

my mum said I never did as I was told
I disagree   it seemed

to me that I had a fully stretched slingshot
ready   set to launch for

everyone I met   that went on
for ages   I'd let fly wear myself

out to try and please
then thunk   my forehead

stoved in   as the pellet I set in
motion   hit the target

true

candle eaters

I stand unmelted in the heat   like a block of jewellers wax   engraved
deeply   with   Chinese   words   their   meanings   escape me

still   I know the trick to looking them up   in the dictionary
my locked box of secrets   glowing commie red up in the bookcase

I am my own   little red book   as full of codes as Turing   he'd be
watching Twin Peaks   he'd be peaking on some acid

envision that Englishman   let
inside my deep prejudice

my English are all liars   eat up children
at the end of sticks   howl over continents in search of souls

to separate   make profit on   they laugh
and not in rooms with drapes of red crushed velvet   like the French

I stand unmelted

all bigotry hard as salt cod   slabbed for export
stupid as a stone

this heart stone   heart stoner   says stone them
action much the simpler thing

than me

crime lords

arresting

stepping over the hedge   the undercovers came
guns pointing forward   the high step took away from

the long charge across the car park   I could see
the child's face   as his hot chips went flying

pulled out of Dad's car   and run run run to safety
or not safety   but that all depends   on where

you stand   where your eyes are   on the day
and all the days   depending

towelling hoods # 1

they wore the hooded towels   that came to pointy vee's
the representing ears   rudimentary   daubs

of colour   paired with some imagination   may be that
    buck teeth
pushed it across the line   so stand before me one
    last time

Cheeper   Buggy   Fluffball the Puddy Tat   and preen
    the paws
rotoscope your carton likeness   wet-footed by the bathtub

before that sagged up grey husk   future whips around the
lintel takes you in his hessian hands   and I feel rough the

way he handles you
towel babies   wet feet on the tiles I slip   I fall   he

puts you in a baby- fight   ring   he pits you
one against the other   next time I

see you it is Cheeper   biting the ear off
Fluffball and the smell of the souvlaki from the

concession van   winter storms bite us
by the old stones of mortuary station

the ring
formed by the architrave

I run

that whole length of the Devonshire street tunnel   wishing
    you were beggars
not fighting on the baby circuit   still with those bunny towels

to pull up on your heads   the small voices
going puddy tat and preening

get back into my   safezone   to let the heartbeats fall
to let the doors slam thick steel   annealed against our

little feet forever walking
ties unsevered   bound

sorter order of the Garter

wanna write the words to make you love me love me
got the heart on fleek again this time maybe this time

all the handsome little soldiers come and lay down   die down   hoe
  down right
at my feet   see   love makes the world go round   I'm drop dead   they
  fly high

as kites   my mummy says the soup kitchen   sells us   crocks of
shit in paper buckets   gets the bums where Uncle Sam

can see us   easier to spot   so stay indoors better starve be safe
my girl   be safe the less love on you the better   fingerprints the

grease   it takes forever to scrub love off   hey the dna alone
will kill ya   and when the whole thing comes to court

the only kinda order get the royal order of the garter
 and she laughs

the Cootamundra tree

cut the centre from
 the tree

it grows   up
anyway   it likes   the

sky   the earth   the air
you come back every year   keep cutting

branches tips
shove the nests away

until the one side of this tree
scarce it can communicate

with the branches down
 the other

near the kerbside
 where the power runs

ants scurry   up and
down   the trunk   the

water flows   up the xylem
 through the phloem   meeting

know the truth
all one tree   you know it
all one tree   leaf tips

distant cousins call

Cootamundra institute of education

this year's guy is better
small fractions count from where I lie

I'm stuck in boxed-up vulnerability
cherry-picker   high   my nightdress   thin batiste

the glass

no barrier but better than the birds
he always comes at nesting time

the linesmen (or his acolytes) to clear
 the way for power   small cheepers

cry out for nil   I wonder if in that other city
my sister's hair is safe

from magpie swoops   hers   the hard wire
of our grandmother   favoured

for the nests   her screams ring
unassauged in time   here the

cherry-picker man scooping out the kernel
of our problem   now

blinds

i/
Morning   brief projector of the silhouetted glory   purple
added later   around noon

when I sink back   scan the painted space above the picture rail
    recalling
dawn   all day one full universe

cosmology and flow   fauna sleeping by the laundry basket full of
lightness dreams

ii/
Letting go the grip
on that   hearsay sun

told retold   here you
make a name   moist

on the skin   made
vigorous with heat exchange

tell me heppalump
get up and move no

five point plan you
boiled star insist

the day constructing relays
failing understanding   wilful

girl   crunches at her lozenge
when everyone   says   suck

Five alarm F

sleep you old attaché case
drop me off at   underwear   again

the time to wake is now now now

gearing up for race day

choose your Chinese father
or your spalpeen mother what

chance the better day

live in town or the river edge
what chance a better

day
after day days come they build like

dam water held back sheer-walled
artistry nothing more than mud
when you crack back to the base

who you gunna choose
on race day
  baby

you can only ride one horse
with that small   gold   arse

unless you want to take it up the riverbank
  with me

make some real
  race day money

this town turns on
  race day
   take your bet

at the Savoy

that light fitting
looks   like a busted arse

see   I made you laugh
 I made you look

and why you crying
girl   anyways they'd never

 get the duster into there
there's me   reluctant

 but the drink
 on the long teak bar   top

sticky ringed says yes   and me
 the one to clean it

you know that   I bet
he wriggled his stool   a bit closer

ahhh
always a girl like you

girl in need

i/
So beat me
 like a rug

down on the rocks   get all the dirt
far-flung   remove the musty footprints all

those visits   tread-marks not made
by you   keep the door mat clean

used to see the ladies in their rollers
bashing them on fences   run

laughing with my brothers   that feels a
century away

I'm dirt and still I'm stuck to you

sentinel

he
always looked so calm always
one dry eye beside the other wry

maybe the mouth   nose never
touched never saw him blow it

pick it wipe it on his sleeve
we will not pass the four bollards of that face

yet press

one hand to his chest there feel that
pale bone cage

rackety with his club-fisting heart
that trapped baboon

in the eye-makeup laboratory
hurling wall to wall blind

accession to the fate   that
 shirt placket like a fire blanket

on a luxury bed

here my heart
one small brown pickled onion

Samsung note

he reached across he put   his phone
in the space   between my breasts

where it quickly cooled   my skin
the very summer of the room   sang out

to all the small vibrations coming from
that dull black case   the shiver of the silver

worn from thumbs   from pants
from careless hurling down

in car central consoles   thrummed back to me
congested   clotted   every minute passing

I served as tabletop   the vanity   while he
stood   tightened   the belt   inserted keys

the wriggle of the tie
stooped to kiss

slid us   both   warm into
the pocket of his suit   goodbye

Gin

I miss the airline tickets
in my email in the morning

calling the accountant saying
can I get some money just until

next Tuesday   now all this
booking on the countrylink

lining up the State Rail   palls   tepid second to
falling into cabs   to giggling fits   who has the cabcharge

and three of them up like flags
in the back seat   divvying up spoils

was worth the rare moments of tedious
explanation   the sniffer dogs going round at

Canberra airport   like moo cows on the Rotolactor
so sure   our luggage will come up trumps

it was the world before   the world before
before the word stopped meaning

you could hold the winning card

not ready for sashiko

(tatewaku)

looking at 'Steam Rising' fresh-stitched on a bookmark how
did I   not see   all the mismatched   higgledy piggledy

stabs in white thread   not
gently rising up   as steam might

fragrant   from a cup of green sencha
recalling   day of silent contemplation   no

this gap-tooth foreigner   just stands at the airport
phrase-book in hand   kimono

sashed across the wrong side
a haystack by a lawn

this spinifex
through snow

lich gates

artisanal glass
architrave of afternoons

you come to me   walking
here on memory's pathway

tent pegs hammered home
the brick clay of

what happened near
the bus stop

 firm as ever
at the doorways

at the gates
in the windows

slighter recollections
wave brightly

turn away

I am set to house-keeping
in the other rooms

hey you

you look the image
of an Irish girl

the beaming drunk on the bus
held out his compliment

the sticky cupcake
between us   at the party

the Irish nun
saw a photo of my son

said he's got that
strong Italian look

I backstroked
the lifting sea

sweet nothings
melting on their tongues

in the mouth
of the beholders

I taste like
chicken

air freight

someone sends me air   it's from America
the north I am afraid to breath it in keep

it locked up in the heat-pressed bubble
that it comes in pillowing the book the swatch

of cloth I saw online wanted pinged over the seas
into my lap   there is this air now this air

from there   stuck here   so far from belonging
the air of punk-arse packers   eking out

a meth head life in trailers no the air of mormons no
the air from canisters spiked with something

made to kill me

I have a box of air now in my shed it is the
air of All Nations   it is sequestered   it leaks through

my dreams it is the leading edge of the cloud that brings
the stormtroopers of the New World Order I rub my eyes

I cannot breathe and still it comes
the air

the inbox

I sent a message it said
tell me how to reach you

message me PM
and you said done

my echo chamber life
the water laps the sky
and it is never done

famous birds and snails

fame must taste like methamphetamine
crack cocaine and the pink in Neapolitan ice cream

to want to keep it on the tongue
all the while hollowing to a corpse

There are no famous birds
giving a shit   at the bus stop   for a good cause

it's for the birds
not this not fame

too busy co-ordinating vision streams
from eye to eye to give perspective

on Facebook trending memes

snails play to the cheap seats
they need the cash

a lot of upkeep on the shells
global warming   yes   it is a snail issue

thank you very much   snail-ist bitch

fame is not a trait of birds
maybe the cassowary

hush   fetch in a magician

sympathetic magic   has a bad rap   under velvet starry skirts
Stevie Nicks   girls with the full hair   and the sullen eyes
it's the sign   you went cuckoo the stamped imprimatur
unreason   sending social scienticians   into cackleberry
squawking

conjure up the centre   for a moment   in the high air
of the seashore   let the birds hold down the corners
of your frail limit
in the combination of those warm-hearted beaks
do not look them in the eye   adding insult to the injury of
your disturbance   hold the minute   complete
evaporation

an agreement never made a bone heal any faster than dissent

did knowledge hidden inside small ladies   sitting rocking by a fire
still add up the same   nothing grew   on the dockets of the supermarket
when the vouchers   all redeemed   got lost
in the graceful swirl of the hair and skin   those dreams your labouring
damn mother   gave you before the stone-air-bird   caw

your symphonic music   took off into the sky   see now
how this   the

taking time to fetch it
down

a trade as moribund as cobbling   yet near to death
  has died

heat is a creature let it fall on me

I can hear these fat cicada out   rioting with pleasure
   under the small trees at Angourie   long time back   ran to find the
    shade

to watch the others prove their manhood   jump-diving off the rock into
   the dark- full
    quarry scoop behind the sea

I can not forgive the green spring rain that fell   sent me shrieking to the
sunlight

 young womanly   revelation   just where cicada pee

ballast

we were   the true
empty lands   scooped and bustled
onto ships

into holds   broken

from earthquakes
river beds   street

cobbles   unwanted
pitched   into darkness

sighing
across seas

salting
the new land

offloaded   rough   on the
offside shore

to whatever
it was

 the valuables
taken

away

know your country

deep roots   fend off heat   those fires that fling themselves cross tree top
to treetop   never pause to gloat on ground obtained below   the

wild hot teeth of fame   see not one finger put   upon the dark black
soil   my encrusting solid cake   of bitter years and fine spring days
    both   worn

to nubs   to wormy flub   for nothing   but this   now this   hate   this
    conflagration
calling birds to fly or die   nothing on four legs   will stand   me
    and my

sly rhizome   fat tuber dull and heavy arsed   I'm plenty
I am planting for the green tomorrow

deep roots   manured surpassing
tree

Stockton Channel ballast grounds

we went down to the ballast ground we took a look around
we found   ourselves   inside the crazy house

of dreaming   nights of sunset   moons of flues
pink baths   small suitcase   with a large false bottom

brought back memories
of my grandfather

coloured cast iron
was the craze

when I was just a baby
or yet born   now

let to roam
the auction sites   lives

imagined
strong

restless in the skin
no hand of mine extended

to the tight-filled form of Bill   or Bob or   Tim the agent
rammed pneumatic into pants and shirt

disembarking four-wheel-drive
a male Jessica rabbit

why are they all so stuffed
like toys without

the fuzz   smooth clean
more than the house was

we fell in love
with the ballast ground   I meant to ask is this

the stones from the
San Francisco Earthquake   the gifts

they gave us
ship by ship

the torn rock pile
shivered up by

quake laden hulls   in trade
but when I saw the agent

well no questions hey

the next door neighbour gave me
frangipani   a white bloom because

everyone wants the pink exotics now
we trembled on the ballast ground

at the freedom   of that land
we wait for Tim Bob

unstuffing in the sun
and we are done

back in class

what's the doing in well-to-do
or is it done already

some time back
a rubber band

pulled back well spent
that sharp snap on your skin

oh
the shiver makes me cry

tell the decades

let the ballast motionless prevail   to take to dust
the stains of latter days   rain fallen gap-roofed

flies dead   stacked five high   always
another piece always another   high   sky high

lie to me lie to me baby   lie to me say   it is
good it is true too true to be real to be sane to be real hot water

that we got into   takes the skin right off   I used to see
the old women   take one ripe tomato from the garden

dunk it with the wire mesh   throw the ball back
skinless   we would strain the seeds out

when it cooled and make passata
talk to me about refined

when the water cools
someday

blue bubble

the little body had no colour to announce the member
race   the blue of the sea had entered

it   a mesh of small holes and slits
emerging as a black lacy wrack extending

from the lower back   like
the sails of bluebottles

she moves the once-smoking man
across   so that his vomit

can't eddy back
onto the corpse

pull him to the hard sand please   she asked
calm as though he had put a book back down

the wrong chute   on return
later at the kiosk with a thin white cotton blanket

across her   against shock she
had a surge of anger   overhearing

someone asking   had the child been
interfered with   as though there was

some greater new
finality left unobserved
why the answer would mean anything
took her right to fury

pay your bills

never think the murderer   a rare bird   needing rifle   sight
   to spy there is one   on every corner   at the elbow

on the barstool   convenience the mantra   of the money
   of the times   sing out elite   law makers   make them
      free   it cannot just be me

Wakefield

(before they identify the body)

it was a Saturday morning   somewhere lay on crumpled sheets
on burned car seats   in stuck down pool of dark red ooze

the work the stuff the next event in some
family story   both   family stories

collide   smashed into wakening   not yet   the coming of the
words the wound   the who where   the why

a long way off today the   cooling body
sticking   gathers in the passion   coalesces blobbing pots for dipping

into horror   pots of holding   still the places
it never will release

concentration

it was obviously him
the round green light

pretending to be her   staring far too long
turn the card again and match

can't reply to email

but can stalk me with another
eye   not any longer do I think

what's up with that
one finger headed to the block function and

I'm told at these moments things click
into place for me there was no discernable sound

 the emotion running smooth in a track worn across
years word matching bitter stinging frightful

all a kids card game
close your eyes turn the card

PTSD

it can't be you   this fear surrounding every move each
eye blink   rethought no   fingers reach from

cold graves   hot fires   alone at night
night just me
moving round the furniture   that distance thins
the way a cervix does   preparatory
to birth once more the scream the push
                     the push the push it
comes to shove   still far along   we
weep out   love's lost husk

crawl   underneath   our
slow thin songs

crime lords #2

I was running this so-called trafficking gig which
meant people called around day in nights out

you wouldn't credit the packets of biscuits
we went through   the flavoured coffee sachets

everyone wants caramel   and leaves their fits on
the cistern   it used to be called dealing   that was in the

time before importance   took a hold and
everybody had to feel   so global   or go home

towelling hoods # 2

in the wet house   where all the dreams
came flying out   in the wet house

her other spaces fell about   in laughing
at the hope of ever keeping sane or getting

far away   in the wet house   drenched by sweat
horror   drips that fall in pins of accuracy   wished up

by a bombmaker   she rides on nightmares   just to make
the coffee   in the wet house   all the walls are white

in the wet house   only she can see   where fingers touched
the walls the floors the small folds of the human brain

meninges   metatarsals singing out   the shrill whistle of the
boiling kettle   tells her   his tea is ready

collapsed volcanoes

I was the small atoll   spaced brown amid
a sea of shallow people all blue with not

having what ever   this year is gunna be
I was the small brown atoll   amid bees   swum

about by fish   thanks for gobbling up the
larvae of the mozzies   now used to coming to

top   here we are locked into this   routine
of feeding   I waken before the clouds

have colour   the sky is sand   taupe   ivory
sky a line mouths wink and gape I am

small

war widow

crossing the road we take the path
of conversation and sudden fire
erupts

play it as it lays
here no folding

this here
can't be under the earth

lest we forget
who stayed to feed the fires

water the yard
not dismiss it
every time

she speaks
her mind

she dies a little
more

panic mercantile

list a hundred things to do   I start to add   I cannot find
the doctor visits   writing poems   moving round the cabinets

sorting out the program for the unsighted   writers for the
next session   I puzzle at the six dot lines   left free

under heading   other   it crushes me with all the weight
that waterfall   that falling   from a great height   torrent   the

meditation   those CD's have been repeating   to me   for at least three
years   an image   that ran off me   literal water off the duck's

back   this now   flat to the stone   splattered   in my-six-dot-space
I am cramming

the work   having never seen before
the line between   what is work   and pleasure   pain   and   well

the rest of it   anything

else   the stuck in the on position   car horn that is
me   suddenly aware   that it is

blaring

collector

it was his favourite knife he said
not thinking   anyone who heard

might draw back reel away
feel pain   he

addressed it as a child
dressed up now in leather

here in suede stands his bride
this knife he got in Rangoon

the late '80's
it is not for display

you know you are meant   to thank
him for the honour of this   audience

once touched   he smiles
you can't resheath this

once you take it from the scabbard
he shows some teeth that might benefit from cleaning off the brown

you have to blood them
there is that tiny bit of drama

the half-centimetre
of knife-steel exposed

yes
like you are going to run me through

as an aphrodisiac on the brushed nylon tiger rug
with your second favourite knife

it's from Rangoon

pits

I rub under my arms   there where
  the heat attracted some giant

octopus to suckle while I slept
  I rise and rinse away the tender

flakes the mouthparts left   I dust
  with sprinkle powder something

anti-fungal then I try
  to stay awake   with fear   against

the long and hungry ribboned-maw
  that monster called the heat wave

look here oh it slouches up the drive

alive

we hide   with
  no success

reassure each other   it will leave
  seek succour cross the chest

wait life

The gold light   after rain   the panting dog   the fan
cicada stilled from long days heat   we
sent slithering   salted
to the ocean baths to the tubs to the
back porch the deep shade in closed-up houses
pumped with chill, artificial air

trees stand still   glad of this   this
turning of the breath   all of us

running together lately
like children do in sleep

in the one long nightmare
in the one long dream

awakened by that storm
now   the last touch of sun sees rosebuds

on my sky   I hold my breath I
rub it like a genie

make a wish

unlock

I kissed your head with all my heart
more than once   in all the years

that came
to chase that day   the day

when you were born my son   I
sneaked in to kiss   again   I was a mother   nobody

could remove that   you glowed   it seemed to me
the key

pills

Maybe you do have
a pill problem   even when

you don't like to take anything
keeping to those six pills a day and

you wouldn't like to go onto something
stronger not when you saw what it did to Craig

those Tramal they stopped working   inside my head
words

maybe you could be a bit more involved
than you give yourself credit for

the quiet carriage broken   rolling out the
back of Cardiff's houses   see there is no view but you

look   the morning glory   and the RX no belay
and bell-like clarity   the opportunity for sympathy

has left me   in the time I took that enema to make this here
trip be possible   one among those clustered small

humiliations   traded for a time-out in the world
and there you are   maybe you do have a problem

maybe you don't   I
say goodbye to the Watagans I strike out
for the Illawarra scarp you

ignorant of the seat beneath your arse

opine on dosages   lament Craig's sad state

sharing wisdom   places you can get a smoke
for free   all the shame is mine   wrestling here inside this

Tree of Life blanket dress   my firmly Buddhist carapace
maybe I do have a problem

I don't like to take   what's here
any more than you do

maybe
fuck me too

fractions

don't go large   be small   be just the one thing
go ahead and do   the one thing   now

ignore the tumult all around   the exhortations
to be global   thinking acting being   ponder not the

ills beyond your touch your scent your sight   find
plenty inside that magic circlet for occupation   high

plains for focus   here   make one thing make one thing
resist the urge to sell   expand   franchise

exponentially become the
abstraction of yourself

if you think
 you can

don't go large
 be one

it ends you know

there is just one more day of life to follow on this road
one sun one moon one meal   to gnaw to gulp to wash and scrape

and moan about to all who cross my smallish sticky path
not so much a glider anymore I drag myself   the sled pushed

forward packed with chattels   of the prophylactic kind   no more
of that tomorrow   rest that finished product   hammock of desires

all day every day
will come

curejoy

We keep improving rooms
our hides this failing life

a truth too simple
not to view as

wilful   asinine the
poverty of spirit

wealth a number
nothing more

translating love
a fulsome race

grow small   grow
small   in thrall

Durrawan

your time of year   has been and gone we look down again
instead of clutching at our heads   waiting for your hair tearing

claws from out the sky that's you Durrawan taking on the postie
he has a hockey stick   inside that crossbar too

too   no Currawong is afraid   of anything   and
I want to be like you

the fairy bread of daytime

time drops
like a plumb bob
  flat to earth   each moment

pulling up
never stops
being   the fascination

the cat opaquely satisfied
holds the roast chicken position
high on a pole   beloved

predator

our land continues
a knotted
up   web of painstaking bargains

every day I
hold out

pod memories   peas
into enamel dishes

I'm Nanna
the day she said
slamming down her cup
drop another bloody bomb on them
after what they done to us

because someone mentioned Noritake
red lipstick   on fine bone chin

lamed forever
  stuck with it

see

I am
my own time lord

 the equator
I am ground zero and

I am stuck with it

not knowing
what I didn't know

changing colours

the fairy bread
is daytime
if you never   think of night

rise

waken in the warm
scent of yesterday's tea
holding to the curtains

woven in the winter mornings
where the raising goes harder

the gristle in me   whinges
I take the crutch
of the blue sky   the black and white peewits

waiting   at the boat ramp
with the coffee
and I rise

Acknowledgments

My thanks go to Varuna for the Dr Eric Dark Flagship Fellowship and Dr Carol Major for her consultancy during my residency, during which I worked on *Know Your Country*